Because I Am Awake

H.R. Shavor

To the people in my life who made this
possible and helped me find good even on
the bad days.
Thank you.

Cover photo credit
Thank you, Don.
For everything.
<3

To you reading this, I hope your good days
outnumber your bad ones. You're not alone.
~H

H.R. ShavorBecause I Am Awake In Bed At 5 in the GD Morning

I lie here,
Awake,
And think of you
And me…
And I wish you were here.
Because I am sore
And you are warm.
Because I'm scared
And seeing you calms me.
Because I want to tell you
All of the things
That my demons won't stop whispering
And the things that randomly pop
Into my head.
Because I am awake in bed
At 5 in the Goddamn morning
I type this instead of calling you
Because I want you to sleep
And I will call you in the morning.
<3

Baggage

It's true
We all have baggage
And some baggage
Is worse than others.
Sometimes I wonder
If anyone else has baggage
That seems threatening...

Losing

Some days
She feels
Like all she does
Is lose.
Like every day
Is a losing battle
And like every risk she takes
Will only end
In failure.
Even when she "wins".

Calm Waters

I stare out at the lake,
Wondering what hides
Under the calm waters.
There are rumors about the lake
And I wonder
Were the rumors founded by fear?
Or something else?

Scared of the Good

She spent so long
Trying
To stand on her own.
Relationships
Are partnerships.
Now that she has a partner
Taking part in her life…
She's scared
Of all the good things
Because she hasn't known good
Like this
For so very long.

Perspective

What might look like one thing
To one person
Might look like something else
To someone else.
Sure
Two people
(Or more)
Can "see" the same thing,
But there's also the chance
That x number of people
Could "see" x number of things.
Perspective
Is…
Well…
A matter of perspective.

Not Once

Not once did I ever think
I'd cry myself to sleep.
Through all the pain
And tears of others,
I was still happy.
By some miracle I was happy.
Then one time,
I cried myself to sleep.
The pain of others,
Their tears,
It all became mine.
Not once I thought I could make this work.
Then he came,
And more like him.
He convinced me I could turn things in my
favor.
Not once did I deny his words.

Our Last Night

I hadn't realized
That night would be our last.
To one,
I haven't missed you for a moment
Since I walked out that door.
To another,
I cried.
A lot.
But I healed.
To myself,
You find the good for everyone else.
Remember to find it for yourself
Now and then
And take your own advice.
To you,
Remember to love yourself.
On good days
AND bad ones.

Broken Wing

Broken wings,
Broken dreams.
How much more can my heart take?
Call out my name,
If I don't respond just send me away,
To a land far beyond.
My heart has no place here.
I belong out there.
You lost me,
When I tore off my wings.

Love Me Anyway

From the start
From you
I didn't hide anything.
My pains,
My hurt,
My heartache…
Everything I went through
And you still ask
All the questions.
You know my past.
And you love me anyway.

Counting Down

They're counting down the days
Until they see each other next.
With every day done
They're closer
To seeing each other,
But more than that,
They're closer to a day
When they won't have to part.
When "bye for now"
Will really only mean
"For now".

Feel the Same

All
I ever want to know
Is that you
Feel the same
For me
As I feel
About you.
Isn't that all
That most of us want
In this world?
To be loved?

Scream

I screamed for you.
You were too good to hear me,
Too good to answer my cries.
While you stand there,
Probably chatting away,
I'm chained to this stone wall.
My memories bite me,
They tear away at me,
Watching me bleed.
They grab hold of you,
And seat you in the chair across from me,
Forcing you to watch.

Blood

I feel it dripping
Watch it hit
The floor.
Crimson stains follow me
Out the door.
They form names
Lost in time.

Saving Myself

I've been so used to saving others
That I couldn't recognize
When it was time to save myself.
Saving myself is the hardest thing
I've ever had to do
And I wasn't alone
In doing it.

I Feel...

I feel like I should shut my mouth forever
And only open to say:
"I love you"
"I miss you"
"I do"
Maybe then I wouldn't slip.
Maybe then I couldn't hurt you.

I hate myself for hurting you.

I wish I could take it back,
But the words have been said.

You haven't replied.
I hope you're alright.
I don't pray anymore.

My head is hurting
My mind is spinning
My stomach is in knots
My wrists... I just won't say.

I'm scared you'll change your mind.
That you'll think I'm too crazy to be the
one.
I'm scared of losing you again
After I said yes again.

I love you.

What more can I say?
I'm sorry for my foolishness
For my fear you'll walk away.
I said I didn't feel worthy,
And someone told me
"You are or he wouldn't have asked you".

I'm scared to death you're hurt right now.
Dragostea mea, please, be okay.

Be Your Tomorrow

I am a lot of things
And there are still more things
That I want to be.
I want to be a good person.
I want to be reliable.
But above those
And above so many other things…
I want to be
In all of your tomorrows.
The good ones
And the bad ones
And all of the ones between
And around those.
I want to be there
For all the things
We don't know what tomorrow
Will bring.
I want to be part
Of your tomorrow.

More Than Once

After her own first marriage
She felt self-conscious.
Like she failed.
But with time
She's learned
So many people she knows
Haven't had just one marriage.
People she looks up to.
She doesn't feel alone.

Black Heart

This void inside me,
This lifeless abyss,
It haunts me.
My light turns on and off.
I cannot see far,
I can only dream.
I dream of what will happen,
And things that happen not.
My heart is not black,
Neither is my soul,
I just thought the title fit.
I just wanted you to know.

They Hate Her

When she left
It wasn't on good terms.
The first thing he did
Was tell his friends
That she did more
Than she really did.
He never let her meet them
And now she never will.
She wonders…
Do they hate her
Because of what he told them?
Did they judge her
Before they ever met her?

Feeling Right

It feels so right
She thinks
As she cuddles up
At his side.
But then…
Her demons start whispering…
And she curls up
As she wraps her arms
Tighter around him.
She's terrified
That one day
This will end,
But for now
It feels so right.

I Won't Apologize

I won't apologize
For feeling the way I do.
I won't ask
That you think
Of all the times you left me
At home alone.
I won't apologize
For wanting to forget about you.

Lost in You

Why do I keep
Coming back for more
And talking to you
Without hesitation?
Because I get lost in you
And our conversations.
I get lost
In the way
That you talk
About your interests
And the way you trust me
With your fears
And your heart.
I like getting lost in you
Because I love you.

Clingy

Your name popped up
In my message list
And I didn't remember you
Until I read through
Some past messages.
I almost got scared
Thinking you'd message me again.
We could have been friends,
But you were my wrong
Kind of clingy.

Distant Wail

Streets away
I hear sirens screaming.
And all I do
Is hope that whoever
They are heading to
Will be okay.

I Was Blind

I was blind
To everything I went through.
I let myself be blind
Because that was easier
Than seeing the truth.
For you,
I was a placeholder.

Meeting You

Before we met in person
We spent hours
Days
And weeks
(Months?)
Sending messages
Back and forth
And phone calls.
Even a video chat.
When I got there
Our hug
Was the best
I'd had in years.

Headspace

Sometimes
Your headspace
Has you at your most productive.
Other times…
It's exactly the opposite.

Go Back

Some days
I wish I could go back
And relive
Some things I survived
Just so I could understand
How I managed to survive those things.
Some days
You couldn't pay me enough
To go through those same things
Another time.

Forever Haunted

In your life
There are things you will go through
That will make you question
If those things
Will forever haunt you.
Those things
Are different for everyone
And not everyone ends up
Being haunted forever,
But there are some people
Who can never shake
Things they've gone through
Or things they've been told.

Old Introduction

You used to stop right by me,
Always time to chat.
Now it seems you just ignore me,
What friendship is that?
Do you remember who I am?
I remember you.
I hear your voice,
I see your smile,
Though it can take me quite a while.
The next time that I see you,
I hope to hear you say,
"You seem oddly familiar,
Have we met before this day?"

How Can I Say

How…
How can I say
All of the things
That you make me feel
When the words I have
Never seem like enough.
Because you…
You are indescribable.
No matter how many words I have
In my arsenal
Or how many times I try to say it
I will always find new ways
To express how I feel for you.
Because my words
Will never do justice
To the way I feel for you.

Blind

When will they see how blind they have
been?
They have ignored their call,
They have seen illusions,
They think they've done no wrong.
They don't know what they do,
Nor can they tell you,
Or me.
We are part of the solution.
That is,
If we choose to be.

Dear Past Me

Thank you.
For surviving everything
Life threw at you.
Even when you didn't want to.
You were NEVER
As worthless as you felt.
You just couldn't see your worth.
You couldn't see how amazing you were.
How amazing we are.
You survived.
Thank you!

He Dared

I sent the first message.
He dared to reply.
We became friends.
We dared to ask questions.
He dared…
To say he had a crush on me.
(I had one on him.)
To ask if we could talk.
(On the phone.)
(I said yes.)
If he could have it on Facebook.
(Our relationship went life that night.)
Since then
We've dared to be happy.

His Party Girl

She's never been the one
Who wanted to go to the bar
Or go out partying.
She's not one for adventure.
He was always one
Who didn't want to be at home.
He'd rather go drinking at the bar.
They've split
And now...
She's with someone new
And she's his party girl
Because their parties
Involve staying inside
And staying up
Watching shows and movies
And playing games together
And talking the whole time
While they cuddle too.
That's their kind of party.

Wearing Out

It used to be
I could stay up
All hours
Day and night
And I was readily available
If anyone needed me.
Now…
I'm lucky if I can stay up
Until 1 in the morning.
My phone is always on ringer
(Unless I'm at work)
So I'm still within reach,
But I feel
Like I'm wearing out
The older I get
And that one day
I won't be able
To help someone in need.

Out of Mad

He went up to her one day
And tried to press her buttons.
She looked at him
And with a smile said
"Sorry, I'm all out of mad today."
He continued to try,
But she just heaved a sigh.
"I told you,
I'm all out of mad."

Just A Dreamer

Growing up
She was nothing more
Than a dreamer.
She had plans,
With no way
To turn them
Into reality.
Now…
She's working five times harder.
Because this time
She's making her dreams
A reality.

Home

Home is not just anywhere,
It's everywhere when I'm with you.
Your laugh and your smile
Make all my pain worthwhile.
Our dreams,
Our secrets,
They bring us closer.
You are the one.
My one to be with,
My one to hold.
You are everything I've seen before,
And everything I love.
In your arms
I know I am home.

Her Own Skin

She sits in his bed
Awaiting his return
And remembers what she told him
The night before.
With him,
She is comfortable
In her own skin.
She's that relaxed with him

His Mistake

His biggest mistake
Was never treating her
What she was worth.
Now,
He has to watch
While others cherish
What he let get away.

Less Traffic

Taking the road less traveled
Can make you stronger,
But there is danger.
In taking the road less traveled
There's no telling what or who you'll meet.
"… way leads on to way"
As Robert Frost once wrote
I find there are few truer words.
Take the road less traveled,
Even though it's not always safe,
In forging your own path along the way
You'll grow stronger as you go.

Experience

Their experiences
Are vastly different.
He has experience with some things
And she has experience with others.
She seeks his advice
And he seeks hers.
They value each others experience.

A Future

I'm looking towards the future
And this time
I'm making plans,
Not just dreams.
I'm not just saying
"One day",
I'm saying
"This year".
My future is bright,
But I won't be blinded.

Unscathed

In the end
I won't be the one to burn
Because by the end
You won't be able
To reach me.
You,
Who so often
Made me feel inadequate.
You,
Who guilted me
For spending time with my family.
After you
I found my worth.
I walked through the flames
And came out unscathed.

Distant Faces

There are names we see
On a phone
Or computer screen
That belong to people
We may never meet.
Sometimes
Distant faces
Can feel closer
Than the ones
You see in person
Day to day.

6.22 Thoughts

I don't know half of what I'm thinking
As I begin to type this down
But I think I hear hearts breaking
Or being thrown into the ground.
Something I never thought I'd go through
Or maybe go through again…
I've made mistakes in my life
And I don't want those to go on.
But you see,
My friend,
Love is love
And love continually moves on.
I question what I'm thinking
And if I really am this strong.
Is this the right decision?
The one I should have aimed for
All along?
Can all the needs get met?
And can everyone survive?

Your Bed

Your bed
Is where we've held
So many deep conversations
And reassured each other
And laughed ourselves silly.
My bed
Is where I fall asleep
When I message you.

More Than A Lover

We started as friends.
I didn't think that we'd be more.
But one night you mentioned
Being too scared to say something
And I told you just say it.
That night we did our first call.
That weekend we first met.
You're so much more than just a lover.
You're one of my best friends.

His Shirt

He sits shirtless
Because I am wearing his.
His choice.
A visual
To remind us
That I am his.

Our Escape

Getting away
Just the two of us
Is our favorite escape.
We don't care where we go
Even if it's running to the store
For normal things.
It's still our escape.

With Eyes Open

I open my eyes
And I see you
Standing in front of me
With that smile
That says you're happy to be there
And those eyes
That show how much you love me
And your hand(s) holding mine
To remind me you aren't letting go.
I don't want to close my eyes.

Pace Yourself

They will tell you to heal,
To move on,
But they won't tell you how.
Only you
Will know
When enough is enough.
Only you
Will know
When you have healed enough
To move on.
Pace yourself.
It is by no means a race.
You know yourself.
Trust that you will know
When you are ready
For the next step.

Walk Away

Know your own worth
And respect yourself enough
To walk away
When there's no hope of change.
Fight for yourself
Because it's not guaranteed
That someone else will.
Even if it hurts
Walk away.

Your Scent

I want to curl up forever
Surrounded by your scent.
I want to feel the warmth of you
Pressed against me.
I want your arms around me
Holding me tight
And never letting go.
Claiming me
Forever yours.

The Other Side

As she sits
And stares at her screen
She wonders
If he still thinks of her.
She's had dreams of him,
Nothing good,
And she wonders
If he ever remembers
Any of the good
They once had between them.
His is the other side
Of their story.

She Doesn't Know

She doesn't know
When she stopped seeing herself
As a human
And let herself be used
As a doormat.
She doesn't know
Why she let herself be fooled
By all the pretty words
When she knows as well
As anyone else
That the shiny words
Can easily be used
To cut your heart
Into tiny pieces.
She doesn't know
When she started to heal
And she doesn't know
When she started to realize these things,
But she's extremely glad
That she did.

She Failed Once

She's had one failed marriage
Already.
And now
When they talk
About a future together
She worries.
She doesn't want to fail again.

Wish I Could Say

There are things
I wish I could say.
But now
Is neither time
Nor place.
Because there are things
I'm sure you wanted me to say.
Too bad.

Almost Lost

She almost lost
All of herself
When she was with him.
When she became free
The truth was clear.
She was hearing things
She should have been hearing
All along.
Things that could have helped her,
But she refused to listen
Because she thought
He was her one.
Turns out
She terribly wrong
And it almost cost her everything.
Her mental health...
Her sanity...
Her life...
All of it.

Persistent Fear

She has a fear
That persists
No matter how many times
He tries to combat it.
Her fear
Is that he
Will one day leave.
Until then…
He keeps reassuring her
That he's not going anywhere
But she's heard those words before
Time and time
Again and again…
Will he be the one
Who holds to his words?

His Tea Skills

I learned a lot of things
When I left my ex.
And there's not a lot I miss.
I don't miss broken promises
And an empty side of the bed
That should be filled.
There is one thing I miss
From time to time.
He could make a mean
Cup of tea.

Hot Fudge Cake

Cold night.
Snow on the ground.
Bowls on the counter
With vanilla ice cream
Waiting.
Timer beeps.
Grandma's hot fudge cake.
Yum.

Knowing Me

Sometimes
I question
Not if others know me,
But if I really know
Myself.

06/17/18

Lying there
In his arms
Post love making
She purrs
As his fingers move through her hair
While she listens to his heart beating
And they talk
About everything.
He teases her
And she responds with a witty remark
And they laugh.
And they watch each other.
And they kiss.
Their hands begin to explore again
On familiar bodies
And they have no regrets about how they
feel
Save for the fact they can't do this all the
time.

Thinking Back

Thinking back
On how things went
I realize…
Everything that happened
Led me to him.
Everything I've been through
Everything I've survived.
It all led me to him.
This man
Who helps me
In so many ways.

Hidden Tears

Tears I shed are hidden,
Not by rain,
But because only two people choose to look.
Hundreds of miles away,
From me,
From each other.
They see clearer than those within ten feet of
me.
I have hidden tears,
I have a past no one really knows,
I have scars no one sees but us three,
Yet I take care of others before myself.
I make sure they are safe before I check my
wounds.

Hidden Marks

Scars and marks
Hidden from sight
Until clothes come off.
Stand in front of the mirror,
See yourself,
Turn around slowly,
Admire the work?
Despite the "artist" of your marks?
Or do you wear them with pride?
Do you share them with someone?
Have you forgotten your marks?
Your past?
Never forget what made you
You.

Autumn Romance

I lie beside you,
Leaves falling around us,
Wind rustling through our hair
As we kiss.
I pray this isn't seasonal love,
But something greater,
Something sent from above.
With my head on your chest
All my fears float away.
I know what I feel,
Because it's you I'm with.
With these leaves floating around us,
The wind in our hair,
And my head on your chest,
I know I'm in love.

Stars Align

Somehow
Stars aligned that night.
It's been our inside joke
Since then.
Multiple messages,
Several texts,
And one phone call.
Who knew it would lead to this?

Shaking The Memories

Try as I might
I can't shake the memory
Of that
One
Damn
Night.
Thankfully,
I've learned to cope.
The memory still
Makes me freeze
And makes it
So I can't breathe,
But I'm learning
To live with it.

Teddy Bear

I snuggle up to you
And every time I do
I can't help but smile
Because at your side
I don't just feel small
And safe.
When I'm at your side…
I feel stronger
And more like the me I want to be.
I guess
The me I want to me
Likes both having
And being
The teddy bear
In the relationship.

Because I Love You

Because I love you
I will not let you fight alone.
I will not always
Be able to be there
But I will
Do my best to be.

She Believed

She believed
That you could change
And that you would
Even though
You never did.
So when the question came
If your marriage
Could be saved
She knew
The answer
Was no.

Be Kind To You

Dear _____,
Be kind to yourself.
You are an amazing person
And you will make mistakes,
Trust me,
But the beauty of being human
Is that we have a lifetime
To learn,
To grow,
To love.
So please,
Be kind to yourself.
You are loved.
You matter.

Hate Me

Even if he hates me
I might not care anymore.
He had his chance
And didn't take it.
I wasn't his partner.
I was nothing more
Than an object he could use.
And when I moved on
He became almost violent.
Some people
Will show you
What you mean to them
When you start seeing
How much you're worth
To yourself
Or when someone else
Shows you what you're worth
To them.
So if he hates me now
For being happy
Then that falls on him.
No one controls your hate
Except you.

Don't Marry Him

If I could go back
And tell myself one thing
I would say
"Don't marry him."

Worthy

I don't know
Who needs to hear this
Right now,
But someone out there does.
Your worth is NOT
Tied to what you can offer someone
Or what you can do for another person.
Your worth
Is tied to you.
The type of person you are.
So if you need to be anything in this world
Be good.

Silence

The silence is deafening
Yeah, the silence is killing me
Because when the silence is there
The voices start to appear
And they're anything but silent.
The voices scream in my head
Saying the things
I fear might be true
That I'm worthless...
Unlovable...
So I question when people say they love me
Because how could they ever mean it?
If I'm not strong enough
To stand up for myself
How can I be strong enough
To stand by someone else?

What to Think

When he messages me
I'm not sure
What to think…
At one point
I thought he could be
A part of my future,
But then…
You vanished.
You didn't remember.
And I moved on...

Through Windows

I remember
Staring out that window
And admiring the view.
But then…
I remember that night.
5 hours was an eternity.

Rumors

Sticks and stones
Can break bones
But words can't hurt you?
Yet the pen
Is mightier
Than the sword
And people hurt themselves
To the point of non-existence
Based on words.
Think before you speak.

Haunting Melodies

Every now and then
You'll hear a song
That stays with you
And not always in a good way.
There are songs out there
That will make you pause
And check twice
And check twice
Before you turn out the light.

A Thousand Leaves

A thousand leaves before me
And all that I can see
Is the endless blue of the sky.
In all that endless blue
All that I can think
Is how sad it is
That there isn't a cloud in the sky
And that I have no one here with me
To enjoy this time with.
There's no one by my side
That I can hug
Or say that I love.
There's no one here
That I can share a kiss with
Because the man who has my heart
Is a few hours away.
And until the one day
When we might meet up
All I have before me
Are these thousand leaves
And the endless blue sky.

Weight Of Words

Before you died
I said some things
To a friend
In frustration.
When you died
I was sick to my stomach
From the things I had said.
As I grew
I forgave my foolish youth,
But still carry the weight of those words.

Months In

Months
Into their relationship
They're comfortable.
The first time they met
They were in shock.
Now…
There's no discomfort between them.
They share all the good
And even the bad.
They know
Their future
Can be amazing.

In a Year

In one year
She went through a personal hell.
But expand it to two years
And while she still went through hell,
She grew.
In those two years
She learned a lot.
About herself
About her family
About her friends
And about self-worth.
Self-worth…
That was the big thing she learned.
Don't let your self-worth
Be decided by another.
No matter who you are
You're better than that.

Let's Pretend

Let's pretend
I didn't go through
The things
That changed me.
Let's pretend
You're not helping me heal
From what someone else
Put me through.

Wake Up Call

She'd had so many signs
But ignored them all
Because she thought
She knew what was best for herself.
And while that might have been the case
Had she paid attention
To any of the signs
She could have saved herself
A lot of pain
And a lot of tears
Among so many other things.
Whatever her wake up call was
She's glad she finally answered it.

Don't Call Me

Don't call me
Those terms of endearment
That you used to use.
You can't butter me up
With your words.
I'm with him
And you're not going
To interfere.
He knows about you
And he knows about how you treated me.
He also know
Things I did
And yes, I told him honestly.
It doesn't stop him
From wrapping his arms around me
And holding me close to him.
My past is behind me.
You can't call me yours.

First Time-Erotic

Hid fingers dance upon my skin
As he begs to be let in,
His lips, so warm, tease my ear
As his breath dances
The fear disappears.

Bodies close as close can be
Not a thing between him and me.
His kiss so soft,
Tongue hot as fire,
Coaxing my own to dance.

With him inside,
We lose track of time,
Our hearts beat
Through the pain
To brand new, sweet pleasure.

The first time of many,
At this point is done.
I could lie here,
Forever,
In his arms, hot as the sun.

Wanted

Once
You wanted me,
But I wasn't enough for you.
We remained friends…
But
It was only after
Someone truly wanted me
You said you wanted me again.
No.
This time,
Someone really wants me.

It Began

It all started
With a message sent
Without expectation
Of getting a reply.
They started talking
More and more…
Months later
They're celebrating months together
And looking towards
Their future.

Theft of Peace

Her peace of mind
Has been stolen
Several times.
By the one who cheated on her
And the girls he cheated with,
By the ones
Who ran off
Instead of talking
About what was happening,
By the one she hurt
Before things imploded,
But...
Her peace of mind
Has only been restored
By the ones she calls family.
The closest friends
And her partner.

She Stands

She stands,
Shakily,
His voice echoing in her mind
Saying all she does is run.
She's still learning to remember
That sometimes standing
Means leaning on those
Who care about you.

My Worst Dream

I wake up
And he's nowhere to be found.
No message.
No note.
He's just gone
And no matter how hard I try
I just can't find him.
I panic
Because my love is gone
And I am alone.

Beyond Amazing

He's beyond amazing.
It's just us,
No one else around.
The thought of his touch alone,
Sends shivers up my spine.
He does things no other can.
Calms the wild,
Tames the beast within me.
He is beyond amazing.

Chasing Dreams

Few times
She feels
Like she's right
Where she needs
To be.
When she's in his arms,
And when she's writing.
Because
When she's in those places
The world
Melts away
And her mind
Is silent.

Borrowed Love

I let you borrow,
But you gave away
My heart,
My love,
The biggest part of me.
How could you!
How could you?
How...

The Right One

Isn't the one
Who doesn't make you cry
Or doesn't argue.
It's the one
Who tells you
How they feel
And makes you aware
Of what you mean to them.
The one who never stops
Because a day with anger
Is a million times better
Than a day
Without you in it.

Unexpected You

I was aiming
To find someone
And I was thinking
I could do it.
But then you came along.
And we started out as friends
With nothing more in mind.
I thought someone like you
Could never be interested
In someone like me.
But then you said something
That took me by surprise
And I was able to tell you the same.
So perfectly unexpected.

How She Feels

He knows it,
But she'd give her all
For him.
To him.
He would do the same
For her.
To her.
They are a team.
They both give their all.
Together.

I Didn't Fall

I didn't fall in love,
I walked into it
Fully willing to accept
Whatever pain that might mean.

Out of Place

She looks at those around her
And feels
Out of place.
She wonders
Frequently
If she
Even belongs there.

Weight of the World

Stop
And remember
To take a breath.
Take a break.
Darling,
The weight of the world
Is not yours to bear.
You are not Atlas
Condemned to carry the world
Forever on your shoulders.
Darling trust me
If you don't take a break
At least now and then
You are going to crack
And recovering from that
Is not an easy task.

Tasting Freedom

That first taste of freedom
Was almost bittersweet.
I was worried
That I was letting everyone down.
I spent so much time
Being afraid.
Waiting for something to happen.
Then I met *him*…
And this taste of freedom
Is one I can savor.

Translations

Words on a page
Or a screen
Are more than that.
They are translations
Of thoughts
Of feelings…
Expression
Isn't easy.

Make You Smile

She knows
Just how to make you smile.
A flick of her tongue
Against your neck
Before she trails soft kisses
Up to your ear.
But you're dreaming
If you think
She's going to
Make you smile
Like that.

It's A Monday

How can you tell
That it's Monday?
When things just will not work.
The servers just keep crashing.
The computers have blue screened.
The phones,
They won't stop ringing!
And to top everything off
Our IT manager is missing!

Done Being Broken

You think she has no trouble sleepin'
But you'd be wrong as wrong could be.
You're all choked up,
But she's not ok.
She thinks about you
Whenever she hears your name.
But there comes a time
Where she doesn't think of you
And she doesn't see your face following her.
There comes a time where she doesn't care
about you
And can help you without it being weird for
her,
But she wonders if it's weird for you
Because you never needed her help before
When she so desperately needed yours.
There came a day
When she had to decide
And she decided
She would not stay broken
Because you
Weren't worth being broken over.

Seeking

They think
They're being clever
But she knows what they're seeking.
They tell her the pretty words
Thinking they'll get her to open up
And do things
She doesn't want to do,
But little do they know
She's been playing that game
A lot longer
Than they have.
She knows the rules
And the tricks
And she's not going
To let them get
What they're seeking from her.

Scribbles By Lamp Light

I'm just sitting here in my room
At 2:30 something A.M.
Wishing I wasn't here.
The numbers on my clock have changed
And they tell me it's a quarter til 3.
My phone vibrates,
I check it, knowing who it is.
I recap an event from 'today',
Though the hours claim it was yesterday.
I look at my netbook,
And the books on my alarm clock
As I debate reading.
Oh, look at that, it's 3 o'clock
And my alarm goes off in five hours.
I stare at a picture,
One I kiss as I go to bed
And as I rise.
Maybe if I stare long enough
My nightmares won't come tonight.

Glimmer & Gleam

Shimmering objects
Always seemed so serene
Until moonlight reflecting off of his knife
Started haunting her dreams.

Just Like This

All she's ever wanted
Was something
Just like this.
They are both
Together
Even when apart,
And she knows she can trust him
With all of her heart.
They are alike,
Yet different
And don't just love each other.
They respect each other.

New Future

I don't care
What his future holds.
I won't be in it.
There's a new future ahead of me
And he won't be part of it.

A Living Goodbye

I knew you
When I was a child.
As I aged
So did you.
I lost a grandmother,
But you lost a wife.
And at that point in your life
Something in you died too.
I didn't just lose her…
I also lost you.

She Sees Herself

She finally sees herself
As worthy
Of the things
That others thought her
Unworthy of.
Things like
Their time
And things like
Her own love.
She's working each day
On loving herself
For who she is
And some days it's a struggle
But she's getting better
With every day that passes.

New Chapter

He tried to keep me down
And he almost managed.
But then…
I gave myself permission
To be happy
Without him.
I reconnected with some friends
And made some new ones.
His chapter in my life is over.
Cheers to a new one.

A Year Later

Almost a year
Has gone by now
And she looks at herself
In the mirror
And wonders
So many things.
If she had stayed
Would she be alive?
Would she have more scars?
Could their union
Have been saved?

A Mistake

There was a night
A man made a mistake
And then a community
Came at him
With nothing but hate.
Working for the community
Was someone he knew
And daily she heard
How he should be lynched.
Day after day
She bit her own tongue
When she wanted to yell.
When she'd had enough
She snapped
Just a bit
And pointed out
Everyone makes mistakes.
Some are bigger than others
And his was a whopper,
But a mistake is just that.
A mistake.

Back Door

I look out the back door
And I can see memories.
Back when he was still around.
At times I miss my friend,
But it was his choice to be gone.
Some walk out that door and never come
back.
After years of coming and going
He left to never look back.
I'll stop missing my old friend one day.

My All

I thought
He was my all
But my world
Did nothing
But fall.

To Forget

Forgetting the bad
Takes so much time
And effort
That she wonders
If she'll ever really forget.
She did love him
Once upon a time,
But there's no way in hell
That she'd go back
To the way things were.
She's moving on
With each day
And with each word
She's healing
Little by little.
Slowly,
She's forgetting.

Story

He sings himself to sleep,
She cries herself to sleep.
They love each other,
Yet neither one of them can tell.
Years later they realize it
And start to try being together.
So much fear between them.
'Will she say yes?'
'Will he try anything with me?'
Questions race through both their minds,
When they admit,
When they realize,
They've loved each other since they started talking.
She hinted to him.
He didn't catch it,
For he was trying to think of how to say he liked her.
Such close friends,
With no distance they can't see,
But once they're apart they realize they knew something all along.
They had a love between them,
That nothing could break.
No relationships could make them forget,
That day they met,
Her relationship problems as he dated her friend,
They talked,
They laughed,

They knew each other's pain,
Yet never realized it.
Something inside them kept pushing them
together.
He invited her to his locker,
When things went bad for him.
That friendly gesture,
Made her head spin,
And caused her heart to jump.
She wanted to hug him,
Like they both did with other friends.
The next year they hardly talked
Outside of a class or two.
She wanted to tell him,
On what she was afraid would be the last
day they ever spoke,
Or saw each other again.
She longed to tell him
"I love you"
But she never did.
She kicked herself
Until they were in contact once more.
When he came back,
They talked more and more.
They shared a secret,
For him to visit friends at school.
They hugged.
They talked more and more,
They hung out with friends,
Their love grew.
She opened her heart to him.
She told him her problem.
Two friends loved her,

One being her boyfriend.
At one point he told her
"I don't want to end up like either of those two."
And she was hurt,
Angry.
Her mother said "He likes you"
And she admitted she liked him.
She wrote him a note,
Speaking of a friend she liked,
But she was afraid didn't like her the same.
All the while,
He wanted to tell her how he realized he felt.
He thought he wasn't good enough back then.
He text her about who it was.
She broke down and told him,
It was he.
He admitted it to her.
She cried happy tears that night.
More confused than ever,
And asked for God's help.
He did years before,
And saw a pair of eyes.
He looked at her picture from a month before,
And she had those eyes God showed him.
She left the one she was with.
He asked her on the way to their first date.
She said "Yes"
And with almost all the tension gone,
They've been happy ever since.
They've feared breaking apart,

But know it won't happen.
They passed the mark where he was scared,
Now it's her turn,
But she comforts him,
And he comforts her.
They say "I love you"
And mean it.
Everything they do,
Everything they say,
Brings them closer.
He leaves sometimes
To go to a job he now never wants to go to.
They know he has to,
And they still talk when he's gone.
They know,
That's all the farther apart,
That they will ever be.

Don't Hear This

I hope you never hear this
Because I don't know how you'll take it.
As much as I want people to read
What I went through
So they know they're not alone
I don't want you to take my words
The wrong way.
Because it could happen.
But I never mention your name
And not all of my words have been about
you.
I write to heal
And if you ever really knew me
You'd know that.
Maybe you'd ever understand that…
But because I don't know
How you'd react
I hope you never hear this.
I hope you never read my book.
Sometimes wondering
How you'd react to my words
Makes me freeze,
But I refuse to be silent.
This is my therapy
And even though you were a part of my past
You're not a part of my future.

Our Song

Our song
Used to be your ringtone
In my phone.
Our song
Got me through
My grandmother's funeral.
Our song
Was a breakup song
Because we thought
We would be forever.
"Even the sun sets in paradise."
Our sun set
But unlike past relationships
I can listen to our song
Without breaking down.
It doesn't hurt
To hear those words
That once meant so much.

Because I Am Awake

Because I am awake
I know I am alive.
I know
That I am stronger
Than whatever comes at me
Because I will keep moving
In the only direction
I will let myself go.
Forward.

He's All That

Is he really all that?
Yeah.
Yeah,
He is.
He's always there.
When I want him to be
And when I don't think I do.
He lets me have my time
And I let him have his.
We have our schedules down
And we have our routines.
They don't always match up,
But we try
And we adjust.
So when I talk about
Just how good he is…
He's all that.

I Found Me

I found myself
While lying in your arms
Listening to you talk
About so many things
And sharing my own things
In return.
I find myself
In the way
You look at me
Even when
I'm being stupid.

Her Broken Self

She stands there
Staring in the mirror
And she tries
To find something,
Anything,
That she likes about herself.
She fails at this.
Her broken self
Is her broken self-esteem.
The voice in her head whisper
That she is always second best,
And she is doing her best
To love herself
After a lifetime
Of never feeling good enough.

What Am I Thinking

You walk back into my life,
And I remember…
All those things you said to me,
All the things we did back then.

I feel your arms slip around me,
Fingers barely touching my skin.
Though I've never felt your touch
It's as familiar as breathing.
When I wake up it's like you're here.

As I fall asleep I feel two bodies
Pressed up to me.
I know those two,
The two that I love.
The feel of them around me
Is more than amazing.

I don't want to lose this,
But something in me says choose.

That something just never says who...

To Stay

She can't wait for the day
She gets to stay.
When there will be
No more counting days
Until they see each other,
Because they'll be together
Every day.

I Want To Go Back

Sometimes
I want to go back
To that day we met
And do things differently.
Sometimes
I want to go back
And spend more time
Doing different things
Like listening to you tell stories
Of when you were a kid.
Sometimes
I just want to go back
And tell myself
It'll be okay.

Real Horrors

She lived
Through real horrors.
And she survived things
That would break others
To the point they couldn't heal.
Entertainment horror?
Is nothing compared
To what she's lived through
And what her nightmares
Consist of.

Fucked Up

All of her mistakes,
All of the times
She stepped out of bounds,
All the times she questioned
If she said the wrong thing…
It's led to her
Being this fucked up
To the point
That she feels
Like that's all she is.
Fucked up.

Moving Forward

He thinks you're nothing
And that without him
You can't stand.
He tells you things
That make it so you can't breathe.
Sweetheart he is lying
Because without YOU
HE is weak.
You are worth so much more
Than he could ever imagine
And one day
You will realize what you mean,
But until then
Keep moving forward.

Almost Missed

In her life
She's taken a lot of shots
Trying to find
That thing called love.
She's found someone
She cares for
Who cares for her
In return.
A partnership.
She almost missed it
For others
Who she wonders
If they only wanted
To take from her
Whatever she had to give.

Could I

Could I walk on the wild side?
Dance with the devil?
Could I lose myself in hell?
I need the challenge,
I want the rush.
No one seems to understand,
Because no one seems to see.
Can't anyone tell?
No,
I guess not.
Could I really chance everything?
All that I've worked so hard
To gain?
Could I?

Through the Tears

That day
A group of us sat
In the kitchen
And talked
About what would happen next.
We knew the road would be long
We knew the road would be bumpy,
But through it all
We managed to laugh
Through our tears.

Do It Bigger

Have you ever been told
To do something bigger?
To make something bolder?
But you knew
That making it bigger
Or bolder
Or anything at all
Was going to make it worse?
And take away from it?
Standing up for your work
Is just as important
As standing up for yourself.
Your work
Is a part of you.
Parts of you
Go into everything you make.
Good
And bad.
Sometimes we can improve
Or expand on something,
But only the creator
Knows when a project is done.

Meaning

She questions her worth
Far more than she should.
She's aware of it,
But she can't help
But continue to question herself.
Year after year
She didn't trust
That her partners meant
What they told her.
Then he came along.
For some reason
She felt the meaning
Behind his words
And she knew…
Every word he said
Was true.

You Broke Her

She sought comfort in your arms…
And your bed…
Hours later
She knows
She made the right call.
You never took advantage
And you broke her
In all the right ways.

Handling Rejection

How she handles rejection:
Tucking her tail
Between her legs,
Licking her wounds,
And moving on.

How her suitors handled rejection:
Anger,
Tears,
Arguing,
Threats,
…

And you wonder
Why she's afraid
Of a raised voice,
Of a sudden move,
…

Dissolve

Most days
You find her laughing
And smiling
And she might be laid back
And easy to talk to,
But when she's at a low…
She's out of touch
And withdrawn into her shell
And she dusts off her mask
And puts it on
So she can cry
And hide
While still being there
And doing the same things
That she does every day
Despite the fact
That she wants nothing more
Than to curl up
And dissolve.

Stupid Deep

My stupidity
Ran so deep
That my heart
Has a gaping wound
That will never fully heal.
That's part of why I write these.
To fill a hole
That's stupid deep.

I Like Me

He might not like me much
These days at least
But I don't care what he thinks
Or what lies he tries to spread.
I like me.
And I like me better
When I'm NOT with him.
I smile more this way.

Missing You

She was the unsuspecting victim
To your love.
She fell for you
And had hopes,
But later on…
Things changed.
Now…
She's worried you won't reply.
She's worried you don't want her now.
The only thing she knows for sure
Is that she's missing you.

Cooking With Him

We don't get to cook together
As often as we'd like,
But when we do
We make a great team.
We trade places
When we need to
And if something needs cleaned
Whoever isn't cooking
Cleans the dishes.
While we cook and clean
We talk
And we laugh
And I think
This is how it should be.

Rewrites

I wish healing
Was as easy
As opening a file
And making the changes.
OR better yet,
Deleting the file.
I would love to rewrite
Certain parts of my life,
But rewrites are rarely
That simple.

Too Many Words

There are too many words
In her head.
She can't get them out fast enough
Because they keep breeding
Like rabbits
Replacing themselves
Faster
Than she can remove them.

Hopeful

I'm trying to stay hopeful.
It's harder than it seems.
I'm trying to stay hopeful
Despite nightmares instead of dreams.
It's so hard to be hopeful
With voices whispering in your ears.
In trying to stay hopeful
I'm battling all my fears.

Moving Through Fog

Some days
She thought she was moving
Through a dream
Or a dense patch of fog
That seemed endless.
Some days..
She still feels like that
Because sometimes
It's all she can do
To just keep moving
Through the fog.

I Knew Better

Something I've always
Been able to say
Is I almost always
Knew better.
Some decisions I've made…
I knew better
Than to make
Yet I still made them.
One of them
Resulted in freedom.
I wasn't sure what was going to happen
When I made the decision I did,
But I'm happier for the result.

Question Mark

When we have something to ask
We say something
Like "Question"
And reply
With "Answer".
It's how we signal
There's something on our mind
And if we're open to answering.
We don't back down
No matter the question.
It's saved us
A lot of anxiety.

Share the Pain

All she wanted
For that weekend
Was to hide away
And sleep.
She didn't want to get out of bed
And she didn't want to speak.
But for some reason she did
And she tried her best.
She worried her partner
He didn't know
She just wanted to rest.
He was worried that she
Had grown tired of him
And she began to worry
He was going to leave.
They reassured one another
Those fears weren't the case.

Dirty Secrets

We have none.
We still have plenty
To learn about each other,
But we hide nothing
And don't pry.
With you
There is trust.

Their Portrait

They had one portrait ever
Taken at a fair
Her parents still have it
On their wall
And she wishes that spot
Was bare.

When I'm With You

I catch myself staring
At your smile
And your eyes.
I can't help it.
I don't have to be "on"
When we're together.
You don't drain my batteries.
When we're together
We're together.

Never Said

I never said
I didn't love you
Even when we were ending
I never said
I didn't love you.
Other things I didn't do?
Stay up at night
Crying over you,
Want to run back to you,
Miss you.

The Last Goodbye

Their parting kiss
Is a vow,
The last one
They will make to each other.
Their parting kiss
Is the vow
That they will stay apart.
It's the one vow
They will keep.

The Words

I just can't find the words to say
How you make me feel each day.
True
I might get shaky
And sprew out all my thoughts
But you tell me that you love that.
Only…
It's not all my thoughts
Or feelings.
Because I can't tell you
Enough times
Or in enough ways
How I feel about you.
You see…
I love you
Just doesn't cut it.

Fight For You

I don't write these
To hurt him
Or get revenge.
I write these words
So I can know it's okay
To forgive myself
For always wanting
To believe the pretty words
And empty promises.

Peel Her Layers

Peel away
Her layers
Until you've reached
Her core.

Love Fully

Even if
It's only for a short time
When you love,
Love fully.
If you don't love someone else fully,
Don't expect them
To love you fully.

Black Rain

Raindrops pour down over me,
So heavily that I cannot see.
These raindrops fall around me,
Pounding the pavement at my feet.
As I look down,
The street turns black.
My tears fall down,
Blending with the rain.
No one sees the inside pain.

Dear Future Me

I'm not sure what to say.
There are questions I want to ask.
Nothing about love
Or where you're at in life,
But things like
Are you proud of me
Or am I making the right choices.
Do you regret having been me?
I'm working towards being a you
That we'll both be proud of.
I hope I'm doing well.

Remembering

There are things
She wants to forget
And some things
She wants to remember,
But those things…
Have mixed together
In her memories.
She can't remember the good of him
Without remembering the bad.
She can't remember the gaming
Without remembering the abandonment.
She can't remember the jokes
Without remembering the tears.
She can't remember the happiness
Without remembering the fear.

Sunny Daze

She doesn't understand
What the big deal is
And why people go crazy
Because the sun is shining.
Sunshine is blinding,
She'd rather have the rain.
At least when it's raining,
She can have her eyes open
More than a crack.
Bring on the rain.

Waste My Time

You say you worry
That you're just wasting my time
Or that you're a burden.
Then waste my time
Because without you in my life
My time means nothing.

Advocate

Life
Gives you two options.
You can either
Stand and fight
For what you believe to be right
Or sit idly by
As the world keeps turning.

Forgiving Myself

I don't write these
To hurt him
Or get revenge.
I write these words
So I can know it's okay
To forgive myself
For always wanting
To believe the pretty words
And empty promises.

Feeling You

I feel your arms around me,
Although you are not here.
I feel the warmth of your love,
Although you are not here
To hear your voice
To see your face
To lie with you,
Basking within your embrace.
You are not here,
For you cannot be.
I know this and yet...
How I wish you were here.

Hiding Her Tears

She's hiding her tears
From him
Because she doesn't want him
To know
How weak she feels
Even if he's the cause of her tears
She still hides them
In her shower.
In her pillow.
In her car.

What I Needed

I keep thinking
Back to how things were.
There were a lot of signs
That should have had me
Doing something differently.
There were a lot of signs
That I should have listened to.
And a lot of voices
Trying to tell me
So many things.
But I didn't listen.
And thinking back on it…
Part of me is glad I didn't
Because it let me make my own mistakes.
And even though I ended up
In an immense amount of pain…
I wonder if going through those things
Wasn't exactly what I needed...

What You're Worth

What you're worth
Is more
Than a text here or there
Or the occasional phone call.
Don't let
"I miss you"
Replace
"I love you"
And
"I'm sorry" or "I'll change"
Or even
"I promise"
Replace action.
You're worth more
Than shiny words
And empty promises.

Can I Spend Tonight in Your Arms?

Can I stay tonight in your arms?
Bathing in your warmth?
Can I tell you that "I love you"
Nah, that just doesn't seem enough.
Can I spend tonight within your arms?
Cuddled close and nuzzled against you.
Forever in your love?
Would it scare you if I asked it?
No matter the answers,
Or what anyone might say
Can I spend tonight in your arms?

Top of Her Head

It's a special place
That few are allowed.
Be it to kiss there
Or rub…
Touch her head
Without being one of her few
And you'll see the demon
She hides
Until it's time to play.

Write the Thing

I don't know
Who needs to hear this
But go write the thing!
I know
You're procrastinating
By reading someone else.
Thank you for reading me,
But
Go
Write
The
Thing.

The Darkest Night

The darkest night
Still gives her flashbacks
And causes her to freeze
When it crosses her mind.
But
It crosses her mind
Less
And less
And slowly
She's healing.

Will There Ever

Will there ever be a day
Where he doesn't cross my mind?
Will I ever be free?
Will there ever be a time
Where I won't need his info
And can finally forget it all?

Blame

You blamed me
For everything.
You probably still do.
Because no matter how much
I did right
The things I did wrong
Were the only ones that mattered.

I Just Want

I just want
To heal
I want one single
Fucking
Day
Where you
Don't invade my thoughts
And make me look over my shoulder.

Hurt Me Right

Hurt me
In the right way
And care for me after.
Be rough,
Be hard,
But afterwards…
Be gentle with me.

Shatter

I'm fighting my bodily urge
To run.
Every day it seems easier,
Yet every night it seems impossible
To keep myself from running off.
I hold myself together
While everyone else breaks down,
But the minute I let go of myself,
I shatter.

The Best Things

Some of the best things
You'll ever experience in life
Are unexpected.
You can't plan for everything,
But you can make the best
Of every situation.

Hold On To Me

Hold me tight
So all my broken pieces
Fuse back together.
Hold me
Until our pains melt away.
Hold me
Until you're sure I won't leave
And I don't question
That you want me,
And even then
Hold onto me.

Nerd Flag

Passions.
Interests.
Hobbies.
Everyone is into something.
So whatever you are into
Fly your nerd flag high,
Wear your nerd flag with pride,
And NEVER
Let anyone make you feel bad
For what makes your heart happy.

To Remember You

I haven't heard your voice
For years.
I can't remember
The sound of your voice
Or how you moved.
I wish I could remember enough
To really miss you.

Until My End

Something's getting in my way,
I'm trying to find my place.
I try to keep myself
From burning these pages I write.
Something has to change.
I feel like I'm wasted,
No clue who I am.
I just continue on,
Until the end.

He Remembers

He remembers
The look on her face
When they first met.
He remembers
The first time
He heard her voice.
He remembers
The important moments
That matter so much
To her.
He remembers
That she trusts him
And he is the one
Who holds her heart.
He knows
How to love her.

Running Away

Running away
From my problems
Has always been something
That I was good at.
But the older I got
The more I learned
That "running away"
Is instinctive.
We retreat
To help preserve ourselves.
The next time I run
It'll be
Because I'm running
Towards an answer
Or a brighter tomorrow.

The Next Step

There will always be
A next step
Waiting for you to take it.
There will always be
A door for you to open.
You can be afraid to do it,
But always take that next step.

Next To You

Next to you
Is where I long to be.
Close enough
I can hear you breathing
As you sleep.
Able to game
On the same screen.
Not having to see your face
On a screen when we call…
I can't wait
Until I'm beside you again.

Tomorrow is a New Day

We are the dreamers.
We are the ones
Who remember the past
Better than others
Because we tie everything
Into our emotions.
Tomorrow is a new day
But that also means today
Is a new yesterday.
Another day
That will be written about
By someone
Who needs to write about it
So they can heal.

What Distance Means

What does it mean
To have distance between
You and the one you love?
It means long phone calls
And multiple messages
At all hours
Of the day and night.
It means video calls
Whenever you get the chance.
It means grinning and bearing it
When your schedules don't line up
And your routines get interrupted.
It means changing your routines
To make sure
You have room for one another.
It means so many things…
But breaking the distance
Means seeing each other
And being able to hold one another close.
Having distance
Means breaking the distance
And proving that love will overcome.

Almost There

The clock ticks by
And in my mind
I relive everything.
How many times
Did I beg for your time
Only to be pushed away?
The worst nights of my life
Were with you.
I'm almost there.
I'm almost free.

She Was Wrong

She was wrong
To do what she did
And she knows it.
She even knew it then,
But part of her didn't care
Because when it happened
She felt more like herself
Than she had in years.
She was wrong,
But she was also
Free
And loved.

Dangerous Lovers

She learned the hard way
The most dangerous people
Are the ones
Who say they love you,
But only want you
For one thing.

Her Debt

Your hands
Don't go on her body
Unless she says they can.
She owes you nothing
So
If you try to take
What you think she owes
She'll prove to you
That she doesn't owe you
A damn thing.

Your Arms

I press my body up to yours
And you slip your arms around me,
Pulling me closer still.

You are warm,
Familiar now.
I feel safe wrapped in your arms.

Here, in your arms,
It's as though nothing bad can reach me.
This is my favorite place.

He Looks

He looks at her
And sees
The stars in her eyes.
He hears her speak
And smiles like a fool
At the lilt of her voice.
Sometimes
He notices
When her voice
Catches
But he still
Looks at her
The same.
With love.

One Step Closer

With everything she does
She's one step closer
To doing things
She's always dreamed of.
This time
She's got a partner
Who cheers her on
Actively,
She's got friends
Who are supportive,
And she's determined.

One Day

One day
You're going to have
So much of me
That you'll wish
For a little less.

9091-89

I used to believe
Anger was poison.
As I've gotten older
I've learned…
Anger is healthy,
Hate is the poison,
But you need both.
Emotions are healthy
When you don't let them
Take control.

Glass Hearts

Glass hearts
Are often
The ones most sought after
And the ones tossed aside
Without a care.
But the thing about glass hearts?
When they're put back
Together…
They reflect the most beautiful things.

Frozen Mind

Some days
Your mind just freezes up
And you can't do anything.
There is desire,
There is want,
But there is no output.
Some days
No matter how hard you try to thaw it
Your brain is frozen.

I've Heard

I haven't seen you lately,
But I've heard some things.
I know these things
Are true
Because those passing the information
To me
Are reliable.
I'm not going to share
What I'm hearing about you,
But I wonder…
If the roles were reversed
Would you offer me
The same courtesy?

The Fear

There's a fear.
A terror.
And when it grabs hold of you
There's no fighting back.
You freeze,
Completely,
And sometimes
It's all you can do
Just to gasp for breath.

Step Back

Some days
You need
To take a step back
And look at yourself
From another
Perspective.
Are you the person
That you want to be?
Or are you nothing more
Than an imposter?
Take a step back
And look at yourself.

Love Her When

Can you love her
When she's falling apart
And can't put herself back together
Like she usually does?
Can you love her
When she finds herself unlovable
And worthless?
When she can't look at herself
Will you be able to look at her
And see her
With love still?
She's terrified
Your answer
Is no.

You Heard

It never mattered what I said
To you.
You only ever heard
What you wanted
To hear.
In the end
You thought I never loved you,
But the truth was
I couldn't have loved you more than I did
If I tried,
But I could have loved myself
A hell of a lot more.

My Words, My Past

My words
Reveal parts of my past
That many people who know me
Aren't aware have happened.
That's because
For the longest time
I hid my words.
I thought I was alone.
I thought I had to fight all of my battles
On my own.
As I grew older
I shared my words
With strangers on the internet.
Probably not a smart move,
But it opened my eyes
To a whole world
Of people who felt like I did.
From then on
I promised myself
That I would never keep silent again.
I would keep sharing my words
And help others know
That they are never alone.
You are never alone.
You reading this.
You are not alone.

Never Afraid

No,
She's never been afraid
Not when he asked
If he needed to kill her too.
Not watching her grandmother die.
Not watching her other one
Get wheeled away.
Not when she got that note.
Certainly not when she almost lost her dad.
No.
Why would she ever be afraid?

Feeling Foolish

Some days
I feel beyond foolish.
Because I want the future
I always imagined.
I almost had it,
But it wasn't what it could have been
Or should have been.
There were a lot of mistakes…
And there were also choices…
But it hasn't stopped me from trying.
And even if I make
A million more mistakes
And always feel foolish
I will find my forever.

dA Fam

Some of my favorite ideas
Have come from people
I've not yet met.
Some of them,
I may never meet
But one thing's for sure
I'm going to try.
I love
dA Fam.
;)

Falling Leaves

Leaves fall around me
As I wish you were here.
Your body close beside me,
Our voices lost in air.
The colors change around us
And we really don't care.
A gust of wind might catch a leaf
And take it flying high,
But what goes up,
They say comes down
And so the leaf will fall.

I Broke

I was broken
When we met.
Still healing
From past wounds
That had festered.
I'm still broken,
But I've been slowly healing
These days
I'm mature enough to know
Someone else can't heal you,
They can only help you on your path.
Thank you for walking mine with me.

Weight of You

I love this feeling
Of lying here in your arms
With the weight of you pressed against me
And your breath on my neck.
It's moments like these
Where the anxiety can't reach me.
Almost.

I Don't Burn

Strike that match.
I don't burn.
Baby after all I've been through
I may as well be fireproof.

The Whore 07.07.18

You let her be called a whore
But the truth is
She sought out love
When she realized
You were never there to provide it.
You ignored her
And you let her be alone
When you could have easily prevented it.
But when she remembered
What it felt like
To be around someone who wanted her
Who honestly wanted to be around her
And when you said "him or me"
You sealed it
Because by that time
She had given up hope
That you would ever be the person
She always thought you were.

Intimidate

You're trying
To intimidate me
But I won't let it work.
You say you could
Pin me against a wall
Easily
Because you
Can bench press
A fridge.
You've got me beat
In strength
And height
And practice,
But I won't
Let you intimidate me
Just because you
Lost your chance
At my heart.

Pink Spoon

When we get together
Sometimes we talk
About things we remember
That grandma and grandpa
Used to have for us.
There was a keyboard toy
That we never mention
Because we always get hung up
On that old pink spoon
Because we have no idea
Whatever happened to it.
Did it get thrown away?
Or lost when they moved?
Whatever happened
To that pink train spoon?

When It's Over

When all is said and done
She knows
She will be able to breathe freely
Because she will have no fear.
She will not care
If she runs into him again
In this life
Or her next one.
He will always be in her memories,
But she will keep moving on.
And day after day
She will think of him less
And less.
Until he is barely
A bad memory.

Back Then

You were already famous
Though I knew neither that
Nor what fame was.

I've known you since I was in diapers.
You are neither friend
Nor enemy.

You are an almost regular part of my life.
While many fear you
I know that you'll touch us all one day.

I didn't know you well back then,
But now,
Now I know you better than I tend to show.

You
Are
Death.

Break Even

I remember that night
And forever I will.
The smooth melody
The vocals that still draw me in…
The reminder that breaks aren't even.
I remember the night I first heard it.
And so well I remember the tears falling
down my face.
I remember all the pain that he caused me
And I carry that pain in my heart each day.
But you learn to live with the pain.
You learn to carry it with you and use it to
help others.
You learn how to protect yourself from that
pain again.
You simply learn.

Survive

I don't care
What anyone else tells you.
You have one job in this life
That's more important
Than any other job
You will ever have.
Survive.

About the writer

I grew up reading and making up stories of my own, but started writing poetry in 2004-2005.
It became my way to process things around me and through writing I've met a lot of amazing people.

Wanna reach out to me?
Instagram: HRShavor
Twitter: HRShavor
Facebook page:
https://www.facebook.com/hrshavor

Made in the USA
Columbia, SC
11 February 2023

11683137R00128